A LETTER

TO A DISSENTER

A LETTER
TO A DISSENTER

Upon occasion of His Majesty's late
gracious Declaration of Indulgence

[By Sir GEORGE SAVILE, Bart.
FIRST MARQUIS OF HALIFAX]

(1687)

Cambridge
at the University Press
1909

CAMBRIDGE
UNIVERSITY PRESS

University Printing House, Cambridge CB2 8BS, United Kingdom

Cambridge University Press is part of the University of Cambridge.

It furthers the University's mission by disseminating knowledge in the pursuit of education, learning and research at the highest international levels of excellence.

www.cambridge.org
Information on this title: www.cambridge.org/9781107453548

© Cambridge University Press 1909

First published 1909
First paperback edition 2014

A catalogue record for this publication is available from the British Library

ISBN 978-1-107-45354-8 Paperback

INTRODUCTORY NOTE

JAMES II originally intended to secure toleration (and supremacy) for the Roman Catholics
by the help of the Anglican Church. His idea
seems to have been a Church Roman in doctrine,
with some privileges of a Gallican sort. Given
the principle of passive obedience then in fashion
among churchmen, they could not logically refuse
to acquiesce in anything he might please to do.
But logic is one thing, practical politics another.
Their fears were roused by the activity and in-
solence of the Jesuit cabal, by the excessive favour
shewn them at court, and by the King's evident
determination to pack the public service and the
army with Roman Catholics in defiance of law.
The breach was completed by the suspension of
Compton (Sept. 1686) and the dismissal of the
King's own brother in law Rochester (Jan. 1687)
for refusing to become a Roman Catholic.

So James changed his tactics. If the Church
would not help him, the Dissenters might. They
had been persecuted of late with unusual severity,
and ought to be grateful for relief. So (April 4,
1687) there came out a Declaration of Indulgence.
In this King James explains that constraint of

conscience had always been contrary to his inclination, promises to maintain the Church, and guarantees all men their lands and properties—the abbey lands in particular. To carry out this liberal policy, he "thinks fit, by virtue of Our royal prerogative," to suspend all penal laws and all tests affecting Nonconformists and recusants (Papists).

It remained for the Nonconformists to make up their minds whether they would side with the King against the Church or with the Church against the King. To help their decision, Halifax wrote his *Letter to a Dissenter* (Aug. 1687).

The present edition is reprinted by permission from Miss Foxcroft's *Life and Letters of Sir George Savile, Bart, first Marquis of Halifax.* Only a few notes have been modified which referred to parts of that work not here reprinted.

H. M. GWATKIN.

November 10, 1909.

A LETTER TO A DISSENTER

SIR,—Since addresses are in fashion[1], give me
leave to make one to you. This is neither the
effect of fear[2], interest, or resentment[3]; therefore
you may be sure it is sincere; and for that reason
it may expect to be kindly received. Whether it
will have power enough to convince, dependeth
upon the reasons, of which you are to judge; and
upon your preparation of mind to be persuaded by
truth, whenever it appeareth to you. It ought not
to be the less welcome for coming from a friendly
hand, one whose kindness to you is not lessened

[1] See Ralph, i. 946, 947, for an account of these. Four of
these addresses, with extracts from others, will be found in the
Somers *Tracts* (Scott's edition), vol. ix.

[2] Ralph, i. 947, quotes Echard as saying that the addresses
presented by a few of the Bishops 'were so jejune and insipid,
that they seem'd rather like the forced Thanks given by a
corrected Child to a severe Parent that holds the Rod over
him,' &c.

[3] 'Resentment: strong perception of good or ill' (Johnson,
definition 1). (It is here probably equivalent to 'gratitude.')

by difference of opinion[1], and who will not let his thoughts for the public be so tied or confined to this or that sub-division of Protestants, as to stifle the charity which, besides all other arguments, is at this time become necessary to preserve us.

I am neither surprised nor provoked to see that in the condition you were put into by the laws, and the ill circumstances you lay under by having the Exclusion and Rebellion laid to your charge, you were desirous to make yourselves less uneasy and obnoxious[2] to authority. Men who are sore run to the nearest remedy with too much haste to consider all the consequences: grains of allowance are to be given, where nature giveth such strong influences[3]. When to men under sufferings it offereth ease, the present pain will hardly allow time to examine the remedies[4]; and the strongest reason can hardly gain a fair audience

[1] From here to the end of the next paragraph should be compared with similar passages in the *Character of a Trimmer*.

[2] 'Obnoxious : liable; exposed' (Johnson, definition 4).

[3] To 'give *influences*' is a very unusual, if not a unique, expression. It is possible we should read 'instances.' (See Johnson: 'Instance, definition 2. Motive; influence; pressing argument; not in use.')

[4] Possibly we should read 'remedy.'

from our mind, whilst so possessed, till the smart is a little allayed.

I do not know whether the warmth that naturally belongeth to new friendships may not make it a harder task for me to persuade you. It is like telling lovers, in the beginning of their joys, that they will in a little time have an end. Such an unwelcome style doth not easily find credit; but I will suppose you are not so far gone in your new passion but that you will hear still; and therefore I am under the less discouragement when I offer to your consideration two things. The first is, the cause you have to suspect your new friends. The second, the duty incumbent upon you, in Christianity and prudence, not to hazard the public safety, neither by desire of ease nor of revenge.

To the first: Consider that, notwithstanding the smooth language which is now put on to engage you, these new friends did not make you their choice, but their refuge; they have ever made their first courtships to the Church of England, and, when they were rejected there, they made their application to you in the second place[1]. The

[1] The wish of James to obtain a toleration for the Papists

instances of this might be given in all times. I do not repeat them, because whatsoever is unnecessary must be tedious, the truth of this assertion being so plain as not to admit a dispute. You cannot therefore reasonably flatter yourselves that there is any inclination to you. They never pretended to allow you any quarter, but[1] to usher in liberty for themselves under that shelter[2]. I refer you to Mr Coleman's Letters[3], and to the Journals of Parliament, where you may be convinced, if you can be so mistaken as to doubt; nay, at this very hour they can hardly forbear, in the height of their courtship, to let fall hard words of you. So little is nature to be restrained; it will start out sometimes, disdaining to submit to the usurpation of art and interest.

alone, in the first place, by working on the loyalty of the English Church, is proved by Barillon's despatches (see Mazure, i. 402), and the expressions quoted from Dissenting sources in Kennett, iii. 462.

[1] I.e. 'Save to.' [2] As in 1672.

[3] Describing the intrigues of the Romish party in the year 1675. They were found, it will be remembered, on his arrest, in the year 1678, for supposed complicity in the Popish Plot, having escaped his notice while destroying the remainder of his correspondence. They were deciphered and published by order of the Parliament; this explains the reference to the Journals.

This alliance between liberty and infallibility, is bringing together the two most contrary things that are in the world. The Church of Rome doth not only dislike the allowing liberty, but by its principles it cannot do it. Wine is not more expressly forbid to the Mahometans than giving heretics liberty to the Papists : they are no more able to make good their vows to you than men married before, and their wife alive, can confirm their contract with another. The continuance of their kindness would be a habit of sin, of which they are to repent, and their absolution is to be had upon no other terms than their promise to destroy you. You are therefore to be hugged now, only that you may be the better squeezed at another time. There must be something extra-ordinary when the Church of Rome setteth up bills[1], and offereth plaisters, for tender consciences : by all that hath hitherto appeared her skill in chirurgery lyeth chiefly in a quick hand, to cut off limbs ; but she is the worst at healing of any that ever pretended to it. To come so quick from another extreme, is such an unnatural motion, that you ought to be upon your guard ; the other day

[1] I.e. advertisements—like a quack.

you were sons of Belial, now you are angels of light. This is a violent change, and it will be fit for you to pause upon it before you believe it : if your features are not altered, neither is their opinion of you, whatever may be pretended. Do you believe less than you did that there is idolatry in the Church of Rome ; sure you do not. See then, how they treat both in words and writing those who entertain that opinion. Conclude from hence how inconsistent their favour is with this single article, except they give you a dispensation for this too, and, by a *non obstante,* secure you that they will not think the worse of you. Think a little how dangerous it is to build upon a foundation of paradoxes. Popery now is the only friend to liberty ; and the known enemy to persecution ; the men of Taunton and Tiverton are above all other eminent for loyalty[1]. The Quakers,

[1] 'Taunton and Tiverton were looked upon as most fanatical places, and their inhabitants had been forward in Monmouth's insurrection. But the citizens of both addressed the King upon the declaration of indulgence, and had been very favourably received.' Note in the Somers *Tracts.* Taunton and Tiverton were the great centres of the West Country clothing trade ; and the trading towns were always remarkable as the centres of Nonconformity. Tiverton, however, to our knowledge, never distinguished itself as Taunton did in 1685. ' Methinks,' says a contemporary critic, ' Hull and Hallifax to a

from being declared by the Papists not to be
Christians, are now made favourites, and taken
into their particular protection; they are on a
sudden grown the most accomplished men of the
kingdom in good breeding, and give thanks with
the best grace, in double refined language. So that
I should not wonder, though a man of that per-
suasion, in spite of his hat, should be master of the
ceremonies[1]. Not to say harsher words, these are
such very new things, that it is impossible not to
suspend our belief till, by a little more experience,
we may be informed whether they are realities or
apparitions. We have been under shameful mis-
takes, if these opinions are true; but for the
present we are apt to be incredulous; except we
could be convinced that the priest's words in this
case too are able to make such a sudden and
effectual change; and that their power is not

Northern man should chime every whit as well as T. and T. of
the West.'

[1] Does this refer to the favour enjoyed at this time by
William Penn? He introduced the Quaker deputation, which
returned thanks in May. The Quakers even condescended to
uncover (*Life* by Hepworth Dixon, edit. 1851, pp. 318, 319).
(See also *Dutch Despatches*, $\frac{\text{April 29}}{\text{May 9}}$: 'And to-day, moreover,
the Quakers, to everyone's astonishment, delivered addresses of
thanks with uncovered head.')

limited to the Sacrament, but that it extendeth to alter the nature of all other things, as often as they are so disposed.

Let me now speak of the instruments of your friendship, and then leave you to judge whether they do not afford matter of suspicion. No sharpness is to be mingled where healing only is intended[1]; so nothing will be said to expose particular men, how strong soever the temptation may be, or how clear the proofs to make it out. A word or two in general, for your better caution, shall suffice ; suppose then, for argument's sake, that the mediators of this new alliance should be such as have been formerly employed in treaties of the same kind, and there detected to have acted by order, and to have been empowered to give encouragements and rewards. Would not this be an argument to suspect them ?

If they should plainly be under engagements to one side, their arguments to the other ought to be received accordingly ; their fair pretences are to be looked upon as part of their commission, which may not improbably give them a dispensation in the case of truth, when it may bring a prejudice upon the service of those by whom they are employed.

[1] By the writer of the *Letter*.

If there should be men who, having formerly had means and authority to persuade by secular arguments, have in pursuance of that power sprinkled money amongst the Dissenting Ministers[1]; and if those very men should now have the same authority, practise the same methods, and disburse where they cannot otherwise persuade: it seemeth to me to be rather an evidence than a presumption of the deceit.

If there should be ministers amongst you who, by having fallen under temptations of this kind, are in some sort engaged to continue their frailty, by the awe they are in lest it should be exposed : the persuasions of these unfortunate men must sure have the less force, and their arguments, though never so specious, are to be suspected, when they come from men who have mortgaged themselves to severe creditors, that expect a rigorous observation of the contract, let it be never so unwarrantable.

[1] This may refer to a fact asserted by Burnet (i. 565), that money was distributed among certain of the Dissenting clergy in 1672, at the time of the first Declaration of Indulgence. Baber and Sir R. Buller, 'who was a famous tool of the Papists afterwards,' are mentioned as intermediaries in a passage quoted from North by Dalrymple (*Memoirs*, edit. 1790, i. 384). For Baber or Barber, see Kennett, iii. 286.

If these, or any others, should at this time
preach up anger and vengeance against the Church
of England[1], may it not without injustice be suspected that a thing so plainly out of season
springeth rather from corruption than mistake;
and that those who act this choleric part do not
believe themselves, but only pursue higher direc-
tions, and endeavour to make good that part of
their contract which obligeth them, upon a for-
feiture, to make use of their inflaming eloquence?
They might apprehend their wages would be
retrenched if they should be moderate : and therefore, whilst violence is their interest, those who have
not the same arguments have no reason to follow
such a partial example.

If there should be men who, by the load of their
crimes against the Government, have been bowed
down to comply with it against their conscience;
who, by incurring the want of a pardon, have drawn
upon themselves the necessity of an entire resigna-
tion : such men are to be lamented, but not to be
believed[2]. Nay, they themselves, when they have

[1] 'Some of them, being penned by persons whom the court
had gained, contained severe reflections on the clergy, and on
their proceedings' (Burnet, iii. 185).

[2] This probably refers to Vincent Alsop, the Presbyterian,

discharged their unwelcome task, will be inwardly glad that their forced endeavours do not succeed, and are pleased when men resist their insinuations; which are far from being voluntary or sincere, but are squeezed out of them by the weight of their being so obnoxious.

If in the height of this great dearness, by comparing things, it should happen[1] that at this instant there is much a surer friendship with those[2] who are so far from allowing liberty that they allow no living to a Protestant under them[3] : let the scene lie in what part of the world it will, the argument will come home, and sure it will afford sufficient ground to suspect. Apparent contradictions must

whose son, having incurred the penalty of treason during Monmouth's rebellion, had received a pardon; to Rosewell, who had been convicted by a packed jury of seditious preaching, and pardoned, but who was bound over to good behaviour during life, under heavy recognizances; and to Lobb, whose name had appeared in the Rye House proclamations. Burnet mentions Lobb as 'an eminent man among the dissenters, who was entirely gained to the court,' and says it was he who proposed committing the seven Bishops to the Tower in 1688 (*History*, iii. 228). All were loud in supporting the Indulgence (Macaulay, i. 229). An address was offered by pardoned men (Ralph, i. 946).

[1] 'Appear' would make better sense.   [2] The French.

[3] This alludes to the Revocation of the Edict of Nantes, which had just taken place.

strike us; neither nature nor reason can digest them: self-flattery, and the desire to deceive ourselves, to gratify a present appetite, with all their power, which is great, cannot get the better of such broad conviction as some things carry along with them. Will you call these vain and empty suspicions? Have you been at all times so void of fears and jealousies as to justify your being so unreasonably valiant in having none upon this occasion? Such an extraordinary courage at this unseasonable time, to say no more, is too dangerous a virtue to be commended.

If then, for these and a thousand other reasons, there is cause to suspect, sure your new friends are not to dictate to you, or advise you; for instance, the addresses that fly abroad every week and murder us with '*Another to the same*[1]'; the first drafts are made by those who are not very proper to be secretaries to the Protestant religion; and it is your part only to write them out fairer again. Strange! that you who have been formerly so much against set forms, should now be content the priests should indite for you. The nature of thanks is an unavoidable consequence of being

[1] They were published in the *Gazette*.

pleased or obliged; they grow in the heart, and from thence shew themselves either in looks, speech, writing, or action: no man was ever thankful because he was bid to be so, but because he had, or thought he had, some reason for it. If then there is cause in this case to pay such extravagant acknowledgments, they will flow naturally, without taking such pains to procure them ; and it is unkindly done to tire all the post-horses with carrying circular letters[1] to solicit that which would be done without any trouble or constraint: if it is really in itself such a favour, what needeth so much pressing men to be thankful, and with such eager circumstances, that where persuasions cannot delude, threatenings are employed to fright them into a compliance? Thanks must be voluntary, not only unconstrained, but unsolicited, else they are either trifles or snares, that[2] either signify nothing, or a great deal more than is intended by those that give them. If an inference should be made, that whoso-

---

[1] On this L'Estrange remarks '(to his Honour be it spoken) never any Man, perhaps, made more Work for *Post-Horses*, with Two or Three Sheets of Paper, then the Author has done with This Letter ; And never any *Letter* perhaps, was more *Universally Circular*, then This has been' (*An Answer*, p. 29).

[2] Or 'they.'

ever thanketh the King for his Declaration is by
that engaged to justify it in point of law ; it is a
greater stride than I presume all those care to make
who are persuaded to address. If it shall be
supposed that all the thankers will be repealers of
the Test whenever a Parliament shall meet ; such
an expectation is better prevented before than
disappointed afterwards ; and the surest way to
avoid the lying under such a scandal is not to do
anything that may give a colour to the mistake.
These bespoken thanks are little less improper than
love-letters that were solicited by the lady to whom
they are to be directed ; so that, besides the little
ground there is to give them, the manner of getting
them doth extremely lessen their value.

It might be wished that you would have sup-
pressed your impatience, and have been content for
the sake of religion, to enjoy it within yourselves,
without the liberty of a public exercise, till a Parliament had allowed it[1] ; but since that could not be,
and that the artifices of some amongst you have
made use of the well-meant zeal of the generality

---

[1] It somewhat lessens the value of the argument, as here
presented, that Parliament, during former sessions, had not
showed the slightest intention of allowing such liberty.

to draw them into this mistake ; I am so far from
blaming you with that sharpness which, perhaps,
the matter in strictness would bear, that I am ready
to err on the side of the more gentle construction.
There is a great difference between enjoying
quietly the advantages of an act irregularly done by
others, and the going about to support it against
the laws in being : the law is so sacred that no
trespass against it is to be defended; yet frailties
may in some measure be excused when they cannot
be justified.   The desire of enjoying a liberty from
which men have been so long restrained, may be a
temptation that their reason is not at all times able
to resist.   If, in such a case, some objections are
leapt over, indifferent[1] men will be more inclined to
lament the occasion than to fall too hard upon the
fault, whilst it is covered with the apology of a good
intention ; but where, to rescue yourselves from
the severity of one law, you give a blow to all the
laws by which your religion and liberty are to be
protected ; and instead of silently receiving the
benefit of this Indulgence you set up for advocates
to support it, you become voluntary aggressors, and
look like counsel retained by the Prerogative

[1] I.e. impartial.

against your old friend Magna Charta, who hath done nothing to deserve her falling thus under your displeasure.

If the case then should be, that the price expected from you for this liberty is giving up your right in the laws, sure you will think twice before you go any further in such a losing bargain. After giving thanks for the breach of one law you lose the right of complaining of the breach of all the rest; you will not very well know how to defend yourselves when you are pressed; and having given up the question when it was for your advantage, you cannot recall it when it shall be to your prejudice. If you will set up at one time a power to help you, which at another time by parity of reason shall be made use of to destroy you, you will neither be pitied nor relieved against a mischief you draw upon yourselves, by being so unreasonably thankful. It is like calling in auxiliaries to help, who are strong enough to subdue you; in such a case your complaints will come too late to be heard, and your sufferings will raise mirth instead of compassion.

If you think for your excuse to expound your thanks so as to restrain them to this particular case, others for their ends will extend them farther, and in these differing interpretations that which is backed by authority will be the most likely to prevail, especially when, by the advantage you have given them, they have in truth the better of the argument, and that the inferences from your own concessions are very strong and express against you. This is so far from being a groundless supposition, that there was a late instance of it the last session of Parliament in the House of Lords[1], where the first thanks, though things of course were interpreted to be the approbation of the King's whole speech, and a restraint from the further examination of any part of it, though never so much disliked ; and it was with difficulty obtained not to be excluded from the liberty of objecting to this mighty prerogative of dispensing merely by this innocent and usual piece of good manners, by which no such thing could possibly be intended.

This showeth that some bounds are to be put to your good breeding, and that the Constitution of England is too valuable a thing to be ventured upon a compliment. Now that you have for some time enjoyed the benefit of the end, it is time for you to look into the danger of the means. The same

[1] November 1685.

reason that made you desirous to get liberty must make you solicitous to preserve it, so that the next thought will naturally be not to engage yourself beyond retreat, and to agree so far with the principles of all religions as not to rely upon a death-bed repentance.

There are certain periods of time which, being once past, make all cautions ineffectual and all remedies desperate. Our understandings are apt to be hurried on by the first heats, which, if not restrained in time, do not give us leave to look back till it is too late. Consider this in the case of your anger against the Church of England, and take warning by their mistake in the same kind when, after the late King's restoration, they preserved so long the bitter taste of your rough usage to them in other times that it made them forget their interest and sacrifice it to their revenge.

Either you will blame this proceeding in them and for that reason not follow it, or if you allow [1] it you have no reason to be offended with them ; so that you must either dismiss your anger or lose your excuse, except you should argue more partially than

[1] I.e. 'approve' (*allaudare*), not, allow, to *grant* (*allocare*) (Skeat).

will be supposed of men of your morality and understanding.

If you had now to do with those rigid prelates who made it a matter of conscience[1] to give you the least indulgence[2], but kept you at an uncharitable distance, and even to your more[3] reasonable scruples continued stiff and inexorable, the argument might be fairer on your side, but since the common danger hath so laid open that mistake that all the former haughtiness towards you is for ever extinguished, and that it hath turned the spirit of persecution into a spirit of peace, charity, and condescension[4], shall this happy change only affect

[1] 'To make a conscience'—'to scruple,' 'to avoid.'

[2] 'Some foolish men retained still their old peevishness. But the far greater part of the clergy began to open their eyes, and see how they had been engaged . . . into all the fury that had been driven on for many years by a popish party. And it was often said, that, if ever God should deliver them out of the present distress, they would keep up their domestic quarrels no more' (Burnet's *History*, edit. 1833, ii. 187).

[3] Or 'most.'

[4] From 'that all the former' to 'condescension,' with the passages 'The Church of England convinced, . . . severe to you,' and 'A general agreement, . . . Common Enemy,' are given by Calamy (Baxter, i. 377) as 'the Marquess's Declaration on behalf of the Church party,' for the effects of which the wiser Dissenters waited. During the debates on the Bill to prevent the Growth of Schism (1703), Montague Lord Halifax

the Church of England? And are you so in love with Separation as not to be moved by this example? It ought to be followed, were there no other reason than that it is a virtue ; but when, besides that, it is become necessary to your preservation, it is impossible to fail the having its effect upon you.

If it should be said that the Church of England is never humble but when she is out of power, and therefore loseth the right of being believed when she pretendeth to it, the answer is : First, it would be an uncharitable[1] objection and very much mistimed ; an unseasonable triumph, not only ungenerous, but unsafe : so that in these respects it cannot be urged without scandal, even though it could be said with

asked (*Works*, 1715, p. 237) whether during the reign of James II. 'it was not owned by some eminent Prelates of the Church, with Archbishop Sancroft at their Head, as well as by the Marquess of Halifax, in his *Letter to the Dissenters*, in which so many Eminent Persons concurred, and which all that Time applauded, that too much Rigour had been used towards Persons of the same Religion for differing in smaller matters ? And whether Promises,' &c. &c.

[1] It is difficult to escape the dilemma, that a similar charity is not extended by the writer to the Romanists. Compare Burnet, 'When some of those who had been always moderate told these, who were putting on another temper, that they would perhaps forget this as soon as the danger was over, they promised the contrary very solemnly' (iii. 187).

truth. Secondly, this is not so in fact, and the argument must fall, being built upon a false foundation ; for whatever may be told you at this very hour, and in the heat and glare of your present sunshine, the Church of England can in a moment bring clouds again and turn the royal thunder upon your heads, blow you off the stage with a breath if she would give but a smile or a kind word[1] ; the least glimpse of her compliance would throw you back into the state of suffering and draw upon you all the arrears of severity which have accrued during the time of this kindness to you ; and yet the Church of England, with all her faults, will not allow herself to be rescued by such unjustifiable means, but chooseth to bear the weight of power rather than lie under the burthen of being criminal.

It cannot be said that she is unprovoked ; books and letters come out every day to call for answers, yet she will not be stirred. From the supposed authors and the style[2], one would swear they were undertakers[3] and had made a contract to fall out

[1] 'The Church had certainly the first Offers, both public and private, and might have had tolerable Terms' (Ralph, i. 948).

[2] Ralph (i. 948, 949) gives extracts from two ; in one he thinks he discerns the animus of L'Estrange.

[3] 'Undertaker'—(1) an enterprising person, (2) manager

with the Church of England. There are lashes in
every address, challenges to draw the pen in every
pamphlet, in short, the fairest occasions in the world
given to quarrel; but she wisely distinguisheth
between the body of Dissenters, whom she will
suppose to act as they do[1] with no ill intent, and
these small skirmishers picked and sent out to
picqueer[2], and to begin a fray amongst the Protestants for the entertainment as well as the
advantage of the Church of Rome[3].

This conduct is so good that it will be scandalous
not to applaud it. It is not equal[4] dealing to blame

for the Court in Parliament, (3) a contractor, (4) a contractor
for funerals. The sense here is probably contractor.

[1] Query : 'to act (as they do) with no,' &c.; or, 'to act as
they do, with no.'

[2] 'Picqueer, a term applied to the practice common amongst
the volunteers and other gentlemen . . . of riding out in front
to fire their pistols at one another' (Wolseley's *Marlborough*,
ii. 237). 'Pickeer, . . . To make a flying skirmish' (Johnson,
definition 2).

[3] 'It was hoped at court, that this fury against the church
would have animated the dissenters to turn upon the clergy
with some of that fierceness with which they themselves had
been lately treated. Some few of the hotter of the dissenters
answered their expectations. Angry speeches and virulent
books were published. Yet these were disowned by the wiser
men among them; and the Clergy, by a general agreement,
made no answer to them' (Burnet's *History*, edit. 1833, iii. 186).

[4] We should say 'fair.'

our adversaries for doing ill and not commend them when they do well.

To hate them because they persecuted, and not to be reconciled to them when they are ready to suffer rather than receive all the advantages that can be gained by a criminal compliance, is a principle no sort of Christians can own, since it would give an objection to them never to be answered.

Think a little who they were that promoted your former persecutions, and then consider how it will look to be angry with the instruments, and at the same time to make a league with the authors[1] of your sufferings.

Have you enough considered what will be expected from you? Are you ready to stand in every borough by virtue of a *congé d'elire*, and instead of election be satisfied if you are returned[2]?

Will you in Parliament justify the dispensing power with all its consequences and repeal the Test, by which you will make way for the repeal of all the laws that were made to preserve your religion, and to enact others that shall destroy it?

[1] This must refer to James II., though at one time during Danby's ministry he certainly declared for Toleration.

[2] The manner in which the Borough Franchises were manipulated by James II. is well known.

Are you disposed to change the liberty of debate into the merit of obedience, and to be made instruments to repeal or enact laws, when the Roman Consistory are Lords of the Articles[1]?

Are you so linked with your new friends as to reject any indulgence a Parliament shall offer you, if it shall not be so comprehensive as to include the Papists in it[2]?

Consider that the implied conditions of your new treaty are no less than that you are to do everything you are desired without examining, and that for this pretended liberty of conscience your real freedom is to be sacrificed. Your former faults hang like chains still about you, you are let loose only upon bail; the first act of non-compliance sendeth you to gaol again.

You may see that the Papists themselves do not rely upon the legality of this power which you are to justify, since the being so very earnest to get it established by a law, and the doing such very hard

[1] The Lords of the Articles were (ostensibly) selected by the estates of the Scotch Parliament, and from this Committee emanated the Bills which were laid before Parliament, to be accepted or rejected.

[2] This probably alludes to the exemption from the *Test*. Halifax was prepared to include the Papists in the repeal of the *penal* laws.

things in order, as they think, to obtain it[1], is a clear evidence that they do not think that the single power of the Crown is in this case a good foundation, especially when this is done under a Prince so very tender of all the rights of sovereignty that he would think it a diminution to his prerogative where he conceiveth it strong enough to go alone, to call in the Legislative help to strengthen and support it[2].

You have formerly blamed the Church of England, and not without reason, for going so far as they did in their compliance[3], and yet as soon as they stopped you see they are not only deserted but prosecuted. Conclude, then, from this example that you must either break off your friendship, or resolve to have no bounds in it. If they do not succeed in their design they will leave you first; if they do, you must either leave them when it will be

[1] This is probably directed against James and his system of 'closeting.'

[2] In the Declaration itself James had rather disingenuously asserted that 'he made no doubt the two Houses would concur with him.'

[3] Compare Burnet, iii. 185. 'And they, who had so long reproached the church of England, as too courtly in their submissions and flatteries, seemed now to vie with them.'

too late for your safety, or else after the queaziness[1] of starting[2] at a surplice you must be forced to swallow transubstantiation.

Remember that the other day those of the Church of England were Trimmers for enduring you[3], and now by a sudden turn you are become the favourites. Do not deceive yourselves, it is not the nature of lasting plants thus to shoot up in a night, you may look gay and green for a little time, but you want a root to give you a continuance. It is not so long since as to be forgotten, that the maxim was, ' *It is impossible for a Dissenter not to be a rebel.*' Consider at this time in France even the new converts are so far from being employed that they are disarmed ; their sudden change maketh them still to be distrusted, notwithstanding that they are reconciled. What are you to expect then from your dear friends to whom, whenever they shall think fit to throw you off again, you have

---

[1] The word 'squeasiness,' which appears in the original editions, is an evident misprint.

[2] 'Start . . . To shrink; to winch [wince]' (Johnson, definition 4).

[3] The sense seems to be : 'those of the Church of England who endured you were Trimmers.'

in other times given such arguments for their excuse?

Besides all this, you act very unskilfully against your visible interest if you throw away the advantages of which you can hardly fail in the next probable revolution[1]. Things tend naturally to what you would have if you would let them alone, and not by an unseasonable activity lose the influences of your good star which promiseth you everything that is prosperous. The Church of England convinced of its error in being severe to you, the Parliament, whenever it meeteth, sure to be gentle to you, the next heir bred in the country which you have so often quoted for a pattern of indulgence[2], a general agreement of all thinking men that we must no more cut ourselves off from the Protestants abroad, but rather enlarge the foundations upon

[1] This passage has been quoted by Ralph (i. 951, 953), very absurdly, as a proof that Halifax already contemplated the expedition of the Stadtholder. It of course alludes to the change which must inevitably accompany the succession of Mary, the 'Next Heir.'

[2] The tolerant policy of the United Provinces was a proverb. Dykvelt was empowered in February to offer a toleration, and, if possible, a comprehension, on the accession of the Princess of Orange.

which we are to build our defences against the common enemy, so that in truth all things seem to conspire to give you ease and satisfaction[1] if by too much haste to anticipate your good fortune you do not destroy it.

The Protestants have but one article of human strength to oppose the power which is now against them, and that is[2] not to lose the advantage of their numbers by being so unwary as to let themselves be divided.

We all agree in our duty to our Prince, our objections to his belief do not hinder us from seeing his virtues, and our not complying with his religion hath no effect upon our allegiance; we are not to be laughed out of our passive obedience and the doctrine of non-resistance, though even those who perhaps owe the best part of their security to that principle are apt to make a jest of it.

So that if we give no advantage by the fatal mistake of misapplying our anger, by the natural course of things this danger will pass away like a

[1] I.e. ease from your sufferings; satisfaction for your aspirations.

[2] Something seems to be omitted here. Query: 'that is a reason, not to.'

shower of hail ; fair weather will succeed, as lowering as the sky now looketh, and all by the plain and easy receipt[1]: *Let us be still, quiet, and undivided, firm at the same time to our religion, our loyalty, and our laws* ; and so long as we continue this method it is next to impossible that the odds of two hundred to one should lose the bet[2] ; except the Church of Rome, which hath been so long barren of miracles, should now in her declining age be brought to bed of one that would outdo the best she can brag of in her legend[3].

To conclude, the short question will be whether you will join with those who must in the end run the same fate with you ? If Protestants of all sorts in their behaviour to one another have been to blame, they are upon more equal terms, and for that very reason it is fitter for them now to be reconciled. Our disunion is not only a reproach but a danger

[1] Used formerly for recipe. (See Johnson, definition 6.)

[2] There seems to be a play on words here. *Odds* being taken in the double sense : first as meaning a simple inequality of proportion ; secondly as a gaming term.

[3] Ralph (i. 951) seems to consider this an anticipatory reflection on the legitimacy of any son James might acknowledge. This is absurd.

to us ; those who believe in modern miracles have more right, at least more excuse, to neglect all secular cautions, but for us it is as justifiable to have no religion as wilfully to throw away the human means of preserving it.

I am,

dear sir,

Your most affectionate humble servant,

T. W.

www.ingramcontent.com/pod-product-compliance
Ingram Content Group UK Ltd.
Pitfield, Milton Keynes, MK11 3LW, UK
UKHW042149280225
455719UK00001B/221